FINDING HOPE
in the
LAST WORDS OF
JESUS

GREG LAURIE

BakerBooks

a division of Baker Publishing Group
Grand Rapids, Michigan

Published by Baker Books
a division of Baker Publishing Group
P.O. Box 6287, Grand Rapids, MI 49516-6287
www.bakerbooks.com

Printed in the United States of America

Library of Congress Cataloging-in-Publication Data
Laurie, Greg.
   Finding hope in the last words of Jesus / Greg Laurie.
      p.   cm.
   ISBN 978-0-8010-7190-4 (pbk.)
   1. Jesus Christ—Seven last words. I. Title.
BT457.L38 2008
232.96'35—dc22   2008038689

FINDING HOPE
in the
LAST WORDS OF
JESUS

CONTENTS

Introduction

FAMOUS LAST WORDS

A number of years ago, I read a newspaper article about opera tenor Richard Versalle of the New York City Metropolitan Opera. During a performance, he climbed up on a ladder for a special scene and sang these words: "Too bad you can only live so long." At that moment, Versalle fell from the ladder and died on the spot. He couldn't have known that those would be his last words.

In every life there will come an end. We all will have a last meal. We all will take a last breath. Of course, we all will give a last statement. We may have the luxury of knowing what our last statement will be. Then again, we may not. No one knows with any certainty when the end will come. I think that we each will die pretty much as we have lived, and our last statements will tend to sum up what our lives were all about.

Such was the case with a very successful businessman who had opened up a chain of restaurants across the country. When his time to die had come, and as his family surrounded him on his deathbed and realized he had only seconds to live, he gave his last words. Everyone leaned forward to hear what he would say. They could barely hear as he spoke in but a whisper, "Slice the ham thin." That summed up his life, didn't it?

Lou Costello of Abbott and Costello had a strawberry ice cream soda as his last meal. The last words he was recorded to have said were, "That is the best ice cream soda I've ever tasted."

History tells of the famous eighteenth-century atheist Voltaire, who was one of the most aggressive antagonists of Christianity. He wrote many works in his attempts to undermine the Christian church. He once said of Jesus Christ, "Curse the wretch. In twenty years, Christianity will be no more. My single hand will destroy the edifice it took twelve apostles to rear."

But Voltaire was less than successful. In fact, a nurse who attended him on his deathbed remarked, "For all of the wealth in Europe, I would not watch another atheist die." According to the physician who was sitting with Voltaire at the time of his death, Voltaire cried out in utter desperation with these words, "I am abandoned by God and man. I will give half of what I am worth if you will give me six months of life. Then I will go to hell and you will go with me, oh Christ, oh Jesus Christ." Voltaire pretty much died as he had lived—miserably.

In contrast, consider the difference faith can make in someone's deathbed experience. We think of the words of the first martyr of the Christian church, young Stephen. As he was being stoned and his life was draining away, he said, "Look! I see the heavens opened and the Son of Man standing at the right hand of God!" (Acts 7:56).

The final words of D. L. Moody, the great evangelist, were: "I see earth receding and heaven is opening. God is calling me."

As we've considered the last words spoken by some well-known figures in history, I want to look together at the last words of Jesus, the most famous last words of all time.

Of course, we know that these words were spoken as Jesus was crucified on the cross. Death by crucifixion was death by suffocation. Although the spikes driven through the hands and feet, the whipping, and all the rest of a crucifixion were incredibly painful, these were not really designed to bring a person to his immediate death. They were really designed to humiliate and torture the prisoner. Death actually came when the one being crucified could no longer breathe. While spikes had been pounded through Jesus' hands and feet, there was a small step at the base of the cross whereby our Lord could push Himself up to get a much-needed breath. While breathing was incredibly difficult, speaking was even more so.

Statement One

FATHER, FORGIVE THEM

As Jesus hung on the cross, He gave seven profound statements. The first of these was, "Father, forgive them, for they do not know what they do" (Luke 23:34). The fact that Jesus' first words from the cross consisted of a prayer does not surprise us. Jesus always had been a man of prayer. Even those who generally refuse to pray will usually do so in their hour of crisis.

But we would have expected Jesus to pray, "Father, help me!" Or, even His later statement being His first: "My God, My God, why have You forsaken Me?" (Matt. 27:46). But knowing Jesus like we do, it was only fitting that He should say what He said in the very order He said it.

He did not pray in that dark hour for His loved ones first, or for His friends. He prayed for His enemies! He modeled exactly what He taught. What He'd spoken one sunny day on the Mount of Beatitudes, He modeled on this very death day at Mount Calvary the words of Matthew 5:44: "Love your enemies, bless those who curse you, do good to those who hate you, and pray for those who spitefully use you and persecute you." Jesus had told Peter to forgive seventy times seven. Now He was doing just that. But when we pray under such circumstances, it is usually for ourselves: "Lord, help!"

When Samson came to his dying hour, he used his great strength to destroy his enemies. In contrast, Jesus showed meekness, which is power under constraint.

We also see from this example of Jesus that no one is beyond the reach of prayer. Jesus was actually praying for the very people who had whipped, beaten, and crucified Him. Talk about "loving your enemies"! Who could have seemed more hardhearted than these people, yet Jesus prayed for them. You may know someone that you cannot imagine being a Christian. Follow the example of our Lord on the cross, and no matter how hopeless it may look, keep praying for that person!

But Jesus also recognized the enormity of their sin, even if they didn't. It was as if Jesus were saying, "Father, forgive them, for they need forgiveness so desperately. . . . Forgive them, for they have committed a sin that is wicked beyond all comprehension. . . . Forgive them, for they have committed a sin that is black beyond all their realization."

When Peter preached on the day of Pentecost, he spoke of the fact that some of those present were personally involved in the actual crucifixion of Jesus Christ!

> "Therefore let all the house of Israel know assuredly that God has made this Jesus, *whom you crucified,* both Lord and Christ." Now when they heard this, they were cut to the heart, and said to Peter and the rest of the apostles, "Men and brethren, what shall we do?"
>
> Acts 2:36–37 (emphasis added)

They were "cut to the heart." This phrase appears only in the New Testament, and it means "to pierce" or "to stab," and thus depicts something sudden and unexpected. It suddenly dawned on them that they had been responsible for the very death of their long-awaited Messiah on the day Jesus died. Can you imagine being guilty of such a thing, to realize that you personally had pounded the nails in His hands?

The One for whom they had longed for centuries, the One who was the hope of their nation and personal lives, had finally come.

Instead of welcoming Him, however, they rejected Him and handed Him over to their bitter and hated enemies, the Romans, for execution. To make matters worse, they realized they personally had done it. Overwhelmed with guilt and remorse, they cried out, "What should we do?" So, we know that this prayer of Jesus was ultimately answered.

Maybe you're praying for someone right now to see his or her need for God. You've brought that friend to church, but there's no apparent interest in spiritual things. Keep praying!

Next to Jesus were two criminals being crucified. It may be that they were more than common thieves, possibly revolutionaries like Barabbas. If so, that means they were militant and dedicated to overthrowing the power of Rome through violence and anarchy.

They were there for their personal crimes, but Jesus was there for the crimes of all humanity. They were there against their wills, but He was there because He willingly went. They could not have escaped, but He could have, with just one word to heaven. They were held to their crosses by nails, but Jesus was held to His cross by love! It's fascinating to see how these three men reacted as they looked death squarely in the face.

Initially, as Jesus was nailed to the cross, the two thieves momentarily forgot their personal pain and joined the chorus of the voices from the onlookers:

> "He saved others," they scoffed, "but he can't save himself! So he is the king of Israel, is he? Let him come down from the cross, and we will believe in him! He trusted God—let God show his approval by delivering him! For he said, 'I am the Son of God.'"

> Matthew 27:42–43 NLT

How this mockery and unbelief must have pained the tender heart of Jesus. Even here at the cross, they persisted. He was atoning for the very people who were spewing this venom.

Matthew's gospel tells us that both thieves joined the crowd in mockery, yet Luke tells us that one of them joined in but was rebuked by the other (see Luke 23:40). Was it a contradiction? No, it was a conversion. Something significant happened to change the heart of one of these thieves, bringing him to his spiritual senses. This one thief had watched with amazement as Jesus suffered the same crucifixion as he and the other, yet without any complaint, angry protest, or cursing. Then He breathed those unbelievable, unexpected, incomprehensible words: "Father, forgive them. . . ."

These words reverberated through the thief's hardened heart. His rebellion, bitterness, and anger that no doubt had driven him all these years dissolved. His heart melted.

Statement Two

TODAY YOU WILL BE WITH ME

The first words Jesus uttered from His cross consisted of a prayer for His enemies, but His second statement was an answer to prayer. It was an answer addressed to one person, and Jesus spoke to him as though he were the only person in the world.

What joy must have filled this man's heart when he heard these words! Also, we cannot help but notice this man's immediate faith: "Lord, remember me *when* You come into Your kingdom" (Luke 23:42, emphasis added).

He did not say, "Remember me *if* You come into your kingdom," but, "Remember me *when* You come into Your kingdom."

It is significant that Jesus said this before His triumphal cry, "It is finished!"; before the supernatural phenomenons of that day; before darkness fell during daylight; and before the veil of the temple was ripped from top to bottom. It would seem at this moment that this thief, who only had come alive spiritually just moments before, had more spiritual insight than any of Jesus' closest followers!

Also, I love the way this new convert defends Jesus to the other thief: "Don't you fear God even when you are dying? We deserve to die for our evil deeds, but this man hasn't done anything wrong" (Luke 23:40–41 NLT).

Seconds old in his newfound faith, and this man is already speaking up for Jesus. That's a lot more than His seasoned followers were doing at this very moment. How typical of many, even in the church today. Often, those who know the most do the least, while those who know the least do the most.

Amazingly, both men heard these words of Jesus. Both saw His flawless and incredible example. Both were dying, and both needed forgiveness. One unrepentant thief died as he had lived: hardened and indifferent. The other repented, believed, and as a result, joined Jesus in Paradise.

The mystery of the gospel! Hearing the same message, one man will listen with indifference while another will have his eyes opened to his need and will believe.

Statement Three

WOMAN, BEHOLD YOUR SON

At the foot of the cross was Jesus' mother, Mary, along with some other women and the apostle John. Can you imagine the anguish Mary experienced seeing her son on the cross? For parents, and certainly mothers, it is exceptionally painful to watch their children suffer.

When my sons were young and they would hurt themselves, it was almost as if I felt their pain myself. I think most parents would take the pain of their children upon themselves—just to avoid seeing their little ones suffer.

Imagine Mary as she looked up at Jesus, hanging on the cross. He was beaten and marred, His body traumatized by the scourging. That was her son. His forehead she used to kiss when He was a boy was now lacerated with a crown of thorns. His hands she once held were now pierced and bloodied by spikes.

As Mary witnessed this brutal event, I believe a statement from thirty years ago rang through her ears. Mary first heard it when she and Joseph took baby Jesus into the temple to dedicate Him. There they met a man named Simeon. God had revealed to Simeon that he would not die until he had seen the Messiah. When Simeon saw Jesus, he said, "Lord, now You are letting Your servant depart in peace" (Luke 2:29). Turning to Mary and gesturing toward Jesus, he said, "Behold, this Child is destined for the fall and rising of many in Israel, and for a sign which will be spoken against" (v. 34). Then he said this to Mary: "Yes, a sword will pierce through your own soul also, that the thoughts of many hearts may be revealed" (v. 35).

Now, what kind of thing is that to say to some woman who is having her newborn baby dedicated? "A sword is going to pierce your soul," he says. But Mary pondered those words. As the years passed by, I think Simeon's statement began to make more and more sense.

On one occasion when Jesus was teaching, someone said to Him, "Look, Your mother and Your brothers are standing outside, seeking to speak with You" (Matt. 12:47). Jesus' reply is interesting. Instead of rolling out the red carpet, He asked, "Who is My mother and who are My brothers?" (v. 48). Then He looked at His disciples and said, "Here are My mother and My brothers! For whoever does the will of My Father in heaven is My brother and sister and mother" (vv. 49–50). Jesus did not exalt His mother. Instead He took the opportunity to stress the importance of doing the Father's will. And the sword pierced a little deeper into Mary's soul.

Now as Mary looked up and witnessed her son Jesus hanging on the cross, I believe the sword pierced all the way through her soul. A new revelation probably came to Mary. Perhaps she realized, for the first time, that Jesus was not her child—but she was His. Maybe for the first time Mary began to grasp the fact that this was not simply her firstborn son. He was God Almighty. It all came into focus for her.

Then the Lord gave His third statement from the cross, a response to what He saw. Looking down at Mary and John, He said to His mother, "Woman, behold your son" (John 19:26). Jesus wasn't referring to Himself here but to the apostle John. He was saying, "Mary, I can no longer take care of you. John is now your son. He will take care of you from now on."

It appears from the Gospel accounts that Joseph, Mary's husband, probably died sometime earlier in the life of Jesus. He simply disappears from the story. Being the eldest son, Jesus apparently cared for His mother in some capacity.

There also existed a rift in Jesus' family, prior to His death and resurrection, because His brothers did not believe He was the Christ until after the resurrection. Now with His approaching death, Jesus wanted someone to care for His mother. This is such a precious picture. Here is the Lord, experiencing excruciating pain and anguish, yet He remembers Mary. Essentially, Jesus was saying, "John, take care of my mother. Look after her. John, I am committing that to you." What a privilege for this apostle who made his way to the cross.

After Jesus said, "Woman, behold your son," He then told John, "Behold your mother!" (John 19:27). From that hour, John took Mary into his home. Even as the Lord hung on the cross, He was thinking about the needs of His mother and her future on earth.

Statement Four

ELI, ELI, LAMA SABACHTHANI?

At noon, darkness suddenly fell on the earth. Piercing through that darkness was the fourth statement of Christ as He cried out, "'Eli, Eli, lama sabachthani?' that is, '*My God, My God, why have You forsaken Me?*'" (Matt. 27:46; see also Mark 15:34).

No fiction writer would have his hero say words like these. They surprise us, disarm us, and cause us to wonder what He meant.

We are looking at something that in many ways is impossible for us as humans to fathom.

Clearly we are treading on holy ground examining such a subject, yet the impact on our lives is so significant, it certainly bears looking into. To Him was imputed the guilt of our sins, and He was suffering the punishment for those sins on our behalf. In some mysterious way that we can never fully comprehend, during those awful hours on the cross, the Father was pouring out the full measure of His wrath against sin. And the recipient of that wrath was God's own beloved Son!

God was punishing Jesus, as if He had personally committed every wicked deed committed by every wicked sinner. And in doing so He could forgive and treat those redeemed ones as if they had lived Christ's perfect life of righteousness.

Jesus accomplished in six hours what would have taken us the rest of eternity to never complete: the forgiveness of our sins!

Scripture clearly teaches Jesus did bear the sin of the world:

> For God made Christ, who never sinned, to be the offering for our sin, so that we could be made right with God through Christ.
>
> 2 Corinthians 5:21 NLT

Surely He has borne our griefs
And carried our sorrows;
Yet we esteemed Him stricken,
Smitten by God, and afflicted.
But He was wounded for our
    transgressions,
He was bruised for our iniquities;
The chastisement for our peace was upon
    Him,
And by His stripes we are healed.

Isaiah 53:4–5

Peter wrote, "He himself bore our sins in his body on the tree" (1 Peter 2:24 NIV).

As biblical scholar Alfred Edersheim said, "He disarmed death by burying its shaft in His own heart" and thereby "death had no more Arrows."

You would think, as a moment like this was unfolding, that the people would stand in complete silence, especially when darkness fell on the earth. But as we read the crucifixion account, we realize that the mockery continued until the very end. Even as He was bearing the sins of the world and crying out, "Eli, Eli, lama sabachthani?" they had no interest at all. People were laughing, mocking, gambling, and acting as though nothing of any importance were taking place.

In reality, the most significant event in human history was unfolding.

I THIRST!

We find the next words Jesus gave from the cross in John 19:28–30:

> After this, Jesus, knowing that all things were now accomplished, that the Scripture might be fulfilled, said, "I thirst!" Now a vessel full of sour wine was sitting there; and they filled a sponge with sour wine, put it on hyssop, and put it to His mouth. So when Jesus had received the sour wine, He said, "It is finished!" And bowing His head, He gave up His spirit.

The fifth statement Jesus made from the cross, "I thirst!" was the first from the lips of our Lord of a personal nature. Scientists tell us that thirst is the most agonizing of all pain. Every cell in the body is crying out for release. This pain only gets worse as time goes by.

Understand that this was not a natural thirst. This was a thirst produced by a tremendous loss of blood. This was a thirst produced by a man who had literally borne the sins of the world. This was a thirst like no man has ever known before. Imagine the Creator of the universe, God Almighty, saying, "I thirst!" The very One who created water was crying out for just a little water to quench this insatiable thirst.

This event reminds us of the utter humanity of Jesus. Yes, at Christmas we celebrate the fact that God became a man. The almighty God became a simple little fetus, was born, and received the nourishment of a mother. Deity in diapers.

It is true that God became a man. But let's not forget that while He indeed was a man, He was not a sinful man. He was a man with no sin at all, yet He voluntarily chose to experience the limitations of the human body. Philippians 2:6–8 sums it up well:

Who, being in the form of God, did not consider it robbery to be equal with God, but made Himself of no reputation, taking the form of a bondservant, and coming in the likeness of men. And being found in appearance as a man, He humbled Himself and became obedient to the point of death, even the death of the cross.

The phrase "He humbled Himself" also could be translated "He emptied Himself." Of what did He empty Himself? His deity? Absolutely not. As the familiar Christmas carol says, "Veiled in flesh the Godhead see, hail the incarnate Deity." Although He humbled Himself, emptied Himself, He did not do away with His deity.

Rather, He did not allow Himself to enjoy the privileges of it. He did not void His deity but veiled it and walked among us, experiencing what men and women experience.

The Bible says that, as a young boy, Jesus increased in wisdom and stature. We read of Him being tired, sleepy, hungry, sorrowful, and angry. These are all human experiences, but with Jesus, none of these were ever sinful in any way, shape, or form. Here, we see Him showing that humanity when He was thirsty.

Is your body wracked with pain? So was His. Have you ever been misunderstood, misjudged, or misrepresented? So was He. Have you ever had those who are nearest and dearest to you turn away? So did He. We have to understand that He has been in a place like many of us might be in right now. He knows what it is like.

He has been there, and therefore, you have a God to whom you can go, a God who has walked in your shoes. He knows what you are going through, as Hebrews 2:17–18 says,

> Therefore, it was necessary for Jesus to be in every respect like us, his brothers and sisters, so that he could be our merciful and faithful High Priest before God. He then could offer a sacrifice that would take away the sins of the people. Since he himself has gone through suffering and temptation, he is able to help us when we are being tempted.

> NLT

When we read these words of our Lord, "I thirst," they remind us of another time when Jesus made a similar statement to the woman at the well (see John 4). He was waiting for her as she came to draw water. She came in the heat of the day, because she was isolated and ostracized from other women in the community as a result of her immoral lifestyle. When Jesus asked her to give Him a drink from the well, a fascinating dialogue followed. He unfolded for this woman the truths of how to know God in a personal way.

When He said to her, "Whoever drinks of this water will thirst again" (John 4:13), He was not only saying that if you drink this water, you will want more in the future, literally. He also was speaking in a spiritual, symbolic sense. Essentially, He was telling her that whatever well she drank from eventually would leave her thirsty again.

This woman had been trying to find satisfaction at the well of human relationships. She had been married and divorced a number of times, and was, at the time, living with a man she wasn't married to. So Jesus proclaimed, "Whoever drinks of this water will thirst again" (John 4:13). In other words, no man would meet the deepest needs of her life. There is no human relationship that will satisfy our inner longings, because we were created to know God.

You can write this over any well of life: If you drink of this water, you will thirst again. You could write it over the well of *career*. You could write it over the well of *possessions*. You could write it over the well of *experiences*. If you drink of this water, you will thirst again. You will always want more.

"I thirst," Jesus was saying to that woman when He asked for a drink of water. Again, as He was hanging on the cross, He says, "I thirst." Here is what it comes down to: because Jesus thirsted, we don't have to. Because He died on the cross, we don't have to be thirsty. He has made possible a way for us to know God. No longer do we have to go thirsting after the empty things this world offers. We can satisfy our thirst in a relationship with Him.

You may recall that prior to this moment, Jesus was offered sour wine mingled with gall—basically, a painkiller. You might also remember that the Lord refused it (see Matt. 27:34). He was going to bear the crucifixion and all of its pain. He would take upon Himself the sin of the world and all of its horror, and He wanted to have full use of His mental faculties.

I have gone under anesthesia only twice in my life. Some time ago, I was having a lot of difficulty with my voice. A surgeon at the UCLA Medical Center discovered a cyst on my vocal cord that needed to be removed. As an outpatient procedure, it sounded simple to me, so I agreed to it. I wanted to get that problem resolved. However, I really didn't know what I was getting myself into.

The day of the surgery, they put me in one of those wonderful little gowns that is so humiliating to wear. As they were preparing the IV, they asked me to sign some papers. I asked what they were for. The anesthesiologist said, "You are going to go under, and you need to sign this so that in case you die, we are not liable."

"In case I die?"

He said, "It is possible." (This anesthesiologist didn't have the greatest bedside manner.)

I was getting a little frightened at this point. "Is it pretty safe to go under like this?"

"It is pretty much like skydiving," he explained. "Most people make it, but some people don't."

I thought, *Is that the best you can do?* I was ready to bolt out of there. After all, this was an elective surgery to help my voice, not save my life.

My wife called for the doctor to come back, and he was very calming. He assured me that it would be okay, and while it was true that it was outpatient surgery, did I want to live with my voice in this condition for the rest of my life? They had done hundreds of these surgeries, he assured me. I calmed down and signed the papers.

They hooked up the IV, and after a few shots from the anesthesiologist, it was lights out. When I woke up, I felt like I had been under for two seconds. Actually I had been in surgery for an hour and a half. I would not have wanted to go through that surgery without being under anesthesia. It would have been a terrifying, not to mention a painful, thing.

Compare that to what Jesus went through, and what I have just described is laughable. There is no comparison at all. Yet He turned away that sedative because He wanted to bear the sin of the whole world. Having done that, and having cried out the words, "My God, My God, why have You forsaken Me?" He then said, "I thirst."

Statement Six

IT IS FINISHED!

I think of Jesus' sixth statement as the battle cry of the cross. Throughout history, certain battle cries have become infamous. When the Japanese attacked Pearl Harbor, their battle cry was "*Tora, tora, tora!*" Patriotic Texans like to remind one another to "Remember the Alamo." When you go to Israel today, they will take you up to a mountaintop fortress known as Masada, where one thousand Jewish zealots lost their lives defending themselves against Roman occupation. They train Israeli soldiers there, telling them, "Remember Masada." These are all battle cries.

This was the battle cry of the cross, the greatest and most far-reaching battle cry ever heard in history, one that the Son of God spoke as He hung on that Roman cross two thousand years ago: "It is finished!" (John 19:30). Those who stood close—Mary, John, the Roman soldiers, and others—were not the only ones who heard these three words. I believe these words echoed throughout the corridors of heaven. I am sure they were heard as a cry of victory among the angels who would have, at any moment, come and gladly delivered the Lord from this situation.

I also think these words reverberated throughout the hallways of hell as Satan realized his plan had backfired. In his blind rage and jealousy, Satan had filled the heart of Judas Iscariot to betray the Lord, but he actually helped bring about the crucifixion of Christ. He unwittingly played into the purpose and plan of the Father, who determined long ago that God would come to this earth in the form of a man and die on a cross. It is spoken of throughout the Old Testament. Suddenly, perhaps at this moment, it dawned on the devil that he had just helped fulfill prophetic Scriptures. He had helped bring about the purposes of God. What was meant to destroy Jesus would now ultimately destroy the devil.

The book of Genesis contains the first Messianic Scripture in the Bible. After Adam and Eve sinned against the Lord, God said to Satan, "There is coming One who will crush your head, but you will bruise His heel." You might say that the battle lines were drawn. Satan knew there was One coming who would crush him. He tried to stop it from happening.

Throughout Scripture, we read of many attempts to stop the arrival of the Messiah. These go all the way back to Exodus, when Pharaoh ordered that all of the Jewish baby boys be killed, on through to the wicked plot of Haman, recorded in Esther, as he tried to have all of the Jews executed. Continuing to the New Testament, King Herod had all of the baby boys in and around Bethlehem killed when he heard there was One born who was known as the King of the Jews.

Now Satan, in his blind rage, had killed Jesus, not realizing that he was fulfilling prophecy: "He shall bruise your head, and you shall bruise His heel" (Gen. 3:15). What did the Bible say about the Messiah? Isaiah the prophet wrote, "But He was wounded for our transgressions, He was *bruised* for our iniquities; the chastisement for our peace was upon Him, and by His stripes we are healed" (Isaiah 53:5, emphasis mine). Sure, Satan bruised the heel of Jesus, but now Jesus would crush his head. This was signified by the battle cry of the cross: "It is finished!"

What does this phrase, "It is finished!" mean? It could be translated a number of ways: It is made an end of. It is paid. It is performed. It is accomplished. Each one of those phrases gives a different facet to the meaning of "It is finished!"

What was made an end of? Our sins and the guilt that accompanied them. What was paid? The price of our redemption. What was performed? The righteous requirements of the law. What was accomplished? All that the Father had given Jesus to do. The storm had finally passed. The devil had done his worst. Now the darkness has ended, and it is finished. Understand, this was a victory cry from Calvary. This was a glorious moment because the work was now completed.

What was finished? Finished were the horrendous sufferings of Christ. Never again would He experience pain. Never again would He bear the sins of the world. Never again would He, even for a moment, be forsaken by God. Finished were the demands of the Mosaic law, those standards laid out in the Scripture that we were unable to keep.

There are people who say, "I don't know that I need Jesus Christ in my life. I live by the Ten Commandments, and that is all the religion I need." Nonsense. Nobody lives by the Ten Commandments. You have broken some of them. I have broken some of them. We have all lied, stolen, coveted, or taken the Lord's name in vain in some way, shape, or form. I have never murdered anyone or committed adultery, but the Bible says that if you stumble in one point of the law, you are guilty of all of it (see James 2:10). These commandments that God gave were not given to make me a righteous person but to show me my need for the Savior.

The apostle Paul summed it up well:

The law of Moses could not save us, because of our sinful nature. But God put into effect a different plan to save us. He sent his own Son in a human body like ours, except that ours are sinful. God destroyed sin's control over us by giving his Son as a sacrifice for our sins. He did this so that the requirement of the law would be fully accomplished for us who no longer follow our sinful nature but instead follow the Spirit.

Romans 8:3–4 NLT

Colossians 2:13–14 says, "He forgave all our sins. He canceled the record that contained the charges against us. He took it and destroyed it by nailing it to Christ's cross" (NLT). Here were all of these laws that condemned us. Then Jesus took the penalty for those broken commandments on Himself.

Satan's stronghold on humanity was finished. The passage I quoted above goes on to say, "In this way, God disarmed the evil rulers and authorities. He shamed them publicly by his victory over them on the cross of Christ" (Col. 2:15 NLT). In other words, the devil was squarely defeated at the cross of Calvary. The author of Hebrews said, "Through death He might destroy him who had the power of death, that is, the devil" (Heb. 2:14). Because of what Jesus accomplished on the cross, we no longer have to be under the power of Satan.

This does not mean we will never be tempted. It does not mean we are not vulnerable to temptation. But it does mean Satan has no rights over our lives. We were under his control, but Jesus paid the price of our redemption. It was as though we were slaves at the auction block, bound by chains, owned by the devil. Jesus came and paid the price for our freedom. This is what happened for us at Calvary.

Therefore, we no longer have to be under the power of any sin if we don't want to be. We don't have to be under the power of immorality. We don't have to be under the power of addiction to drugs or alcohol. We don't have to be under the power of any vice or any lifestyle. We have been freed by what Jesus did on the cross. He has opened the door to our prison cells, but each of us must get up and walk out.

Remember the story in Acts 12, when Peter was in prison and the believers prayed for him? An angel of the Lord was sent to deliver him, and the door of the prison was opened. But Peter had to walk out that door.

Some of us don't want to be freed from the vice that is strangling us. Some of us don't want to change. Some of us don't want to get out of the darkness we are in. I am telling you on the authority of Scripture that if you want out, the door is open. Jesus Christ has paid the price. He has already made available to you the power and the resources to be victorious over the power of sin. Your life may not be sinless, but you can sin less. Your life can be transformed because of what was finished on the cross.

Finished was our salvation. All our sins were transferred to Jesus when He hung on the cross, and righteousness was transferred to our account. As Isaiah 53:6 says, "The Lord has laid on Him the iniquity of us all." It is finished! There is nothing that you or I can add to the work that Jesus accomplished for us.

Sometimes we think it is necessary to earn our salvation with certain good works. But Jesus said, "It is finished!" God Almighty is satisfied with the work of Christ. Are you? There is nothing you can add to it. It has all been paid. As the hymn says, "Jesus paid it all, / All to Him I owe; / Sin had left a crimson stain, / He washed it white as snow." It is all paid—no more debts left. Jesus has done this for you and for me. "It is finished!"

INTO YOUR HANDS
I COMMIT MY SPIRIT

Jesus then gives His seventh and final statement from the cross. He says to the Father, "Into Your hands I commit My spirit" (Luke 23:46). Earlier on, the Lord had said, "No one takes it [My life] from Me, but I lay it down of Myself. I have power to lay it down, and I have power to take it again" (John 10:18). The Roman soldiers who came to break Jesus' legs were amazed He had already died. This practice was intended to prevent the one on the cross from pulling up for a breath. As a result, the prisoner would immediately die of suffocation. When they came to Jesus, it was not necessary to break His bones, which fulfilled the Scripture that says not one of His bones would be broken (see Exod. 12:46; Num. 9:12; Ps. 34:20; John 19:36).

Many significant events took place when Jesus died. Three of the Gospels tell us that the veil in the temple was torn in two, from top to bottom (Matt. 27:51; Mark 15:38; Luke 23:45). Some thirty-six inches thick, this veil was tightly woven, forming a wall of material that separated the Holy of Holies from the other sections of the temple. It was this inner sanctum that the priests entered once a year on the Day of Atonement to offer a sacrifice for the sins of the people.

Can you imagine all of the worshipers in the temple at that moment? Suddenly, that huge veil began to tear, not from the bottom to the top as though a person was ripping it, but from top to bottom. God was saying, "There is no longer a wall keeping you from access to Me. The barrier is removed." By ripping the temple veil, God was, in effect, saying that through the death of His Son, we can have total access into His presence, twenty-four hours a day, seven days a week. We don't need a priest or anyone else to represent us. We can come to Him at any time through His Son Jesus Christ. As Hebrews 10:19–22 says,

Therefore, brethren, having boldness to enter the Holiest by the blood of Jesus, by a new and living way which He consecrated for us, through the veil, that is, His flesh, and having a High Priest over the house of God, let us draw near with a true heart in full assurance of faith.

Following the crucifixion of Jesus, Joseph of Arimathea, a secret follower of His, asked Pilate for permission to take away Jesus' body. Having received permission, Joseph, along with Nicodemus, who came with about one hundred pounds of myrrh and aloe (see John 19:38–39), took the body of Jesus and prepared it for burial.

We find Nicodemus's story in John 3. He approached Jesus at night, presumably because he was afraid of being seen. Nicodemus, a well-known spiritual leader in the nation of Israel, was intrigued by the message of Christ. He came to Jesus undercover, wanting to hear what He had to say. The Lord asked him, "Are you the teacher of Israel, and do not know these things?" (John 3:10). Nicodemus was a spiritual leader. He was the one others looked to. Yet Nicodemus was asking Jesus how to know God. Jesus told him, "You must be born again" (John 3:7).

We don't read that Nicodemus believed at that point. Obviously, he believed then or sometime later. Now, in the end, he came through for the Lord. It is true that he came to Jesus by night, but it is also true that he stood with Him in the end. Nicodemus turned out to be one of the bravest followers of Christ.

Keep in mind that in everything, there must be a beginning. Some have a great beginning with Jesus, only to deny Him later. For instance, Judas Iscariot was an apostle in the early days of Jesus' ministry. Yet at the end of our Lord's ministry, he betrayed Jesus and went and hung himself. Nicodemus stepped forward when all of the disciples forsook Him and fled.

Life is full of surprises. As I think back thirty-eight years to when I first became a Christian, I remember those who were walking with the Lord at the time. A number of those people are not walking with Him today. There were certain people back then who I thought would make their mark for the kingdom of God, and they did not. On the other hand, I think of others who I thought would never make it, and they have.

I believe there will be three big surprises when we get to heaven: One, a lot of people we thought would be there will not be. Two, a lot of the people we never thought would be there will be. And three, we will be there. My point is, you can have a great beginning and a horrible ending. Just because you start well doesn't mean you will finish well. However, you can have both a great beginning and a wonderful ending. You also can have a feeble beginning and a glorious ending.

Look at Nicodemus, for example. You might say that he had a feeble beginning. He secretly came to Jesus by night for fear of what others would think. Look at him now. Where are Peter and James? Who knows? Where is the rest of the gang? *Hiding*.

Where is Nicodemus? Out front and center, saying he will take the body of Jesus. He was a famous and well-known man. But he wanted to stand up for the Lord. We need to think about that. Maybe some of us have not been doing so well spiritually. We might be limping along. The good news is you can make a recommitment to finish well. You still can try, to the best of your ability, to make up for lost time.

One day, you will take your last breath. You will eat your last meal. You will speak your final words. The apostle Paul recognized this. Knowing his life was coming to a close, he wrote these words:

I have fought the good fight, I have finished the race, I have kept the faith. Finally, there is laid up for me the crown of righteousness, which the Lord, the righteous Judge, will give to me on that Day, and not to me only but also to all who have loved His appearing.

2 Timothy 4:7–8

Paul was saying that he finished the race he had begun. Will you be able to say that? If not, you can make a change now. I think of the words of the author of Hebrews:

Therefore we also, since we are surrounded by so great a cloud of witnesses, let us lay aside every weight, and the sin which so easily ensnares us, and let us run with endurance the race that is set before us, looking unto Jesus, the author and finisher of our faith, who for the joy that was set before Him endured the cross, despising the shame, and has sat down at the right hand of the throne of God.

Hebrews 12:1–2

Keep running the race and look to Jesus. Consider what He went through for you. You can go through this for Him. He is the author and finisher of your faith. What God begins, He wants to finish. But you need to cooperate. You need to want that as well. You need to be working together with Him.

Paul the apostle told the Christians in Philippi, "Work out your own salvation with fear and trembling" (Phil. 2:12). Sometimes we read a verse like that and think it contradicts the statement I made earlier about Jesus paying for our salvation on the cross. What does it mean "to work it out"? It means to carry it to the goal, fully complete. It doesn't mean you earn it or pay for it. It means that God has given you this salvation. Now carry it to the goal, fully complete. Let it become your life.

Then that verse continues on and says, "For it is God who works in you both to will and to do for His good pleasure" (Phil. 2:13). It is not that I'm doing it in my own strength. It is God working through me, completing the work He has begun.

It is finished! He finished it for you. Now will you finish this race for Him? Even if you have not started well, you can still finish well. Even if you have limped up to this point, you can get up and get back in the race again. Even if you have fallen, there is forgiveness, but you need to ask God for it. Recommit yourself to finish well.

The Power
of Christ's Words

Christ made His love for the world passionately evident in His statements from the cross, and the presentation of these statements in all of their pain, victory, and meaning is powerful to behold:

Statement One

"Father, forgive them for they know not what they do."

Do you realize that you are in need of the Father's forgiveness?

Statement Two

"Today you will be with Me in Paradise."

Have you realized and confessed Jesus as your personal Savior?

Statement Three

"Woman, behold your son."

Jesus is concerned for us and provides for all of us.

Statement Four

"My God, My God, why have You forsaken Me?"

Jesus was forsaken so we don't have to be.

Statement Five

"I thirst!"

This personal statement reminds us that Jesus is not only God, but He also was man. Jesus identifies with our needs.

Statement Six

"It is finished!"

Jesus paid for our sins, and sin's control over our lives is broken!

Statement Seven

"Into Your hands I commit My spirit."

You can entrust your life into God's hands.

Maybe you're reading this today and you've never committed your life to Jesus Christ. You don't know His forgiveness. You don't have the assurance that if you died, you would go to heaven. Why don't you confess Jesus as Lord and Savior of your life? If you do, you will be forgiven of all your sins. You can finish well and know that you will go to heaven. If you need His forgiveness, if you need to place your faith in Jesus Christ, then do it before this day is over. Why not take a moment right now and say a prayer like this one:

Lord Jesus, I know that I am a sinner, and I am sorry for my sin. I repent of it and turn to You by faith right now. I thank You for dying on the cross for me and paying the price for all of my sins. Thank You for rising from the dead as well. I ask You to come into my life right now and be my Lord, my Savior, and my friend. Fill me with Your Holy Spirit. Help me to be Your disciple from this moment forward. Thank You, Lord. In Jesus' name I pray. Amen.

Dear Friend,

If you prayed to receive Jesus Christ as Lord and Savior while reading this book, then you have now begun a lifelong, personal relationship with Him. Your decision to follow Christ means God has forgiven you and that you will spend eternity in heaven with Him. The Bible tells us, "If we confess our sins, He is faithful and just to forgive us our sins and to cleanse us from all unrighteousness" (1 John 1:9).

To put your faith in action, be sure to connect with a Bible-believing church in your area. Spend time with God by reading the Bible, praying, going to church, and telling others about Christ.

May God bless you as you grow closer to Him.

ALSO BY
GREG LAURIE

**Walking with Jesus:
Daily Inspiration from
the Gospel of John**
978-0-8010-6815-7
$12.99

Beloved pastor and author Greg Laurie helps you spend time with Jesus in this inspiring devotional. Perfect for a regular time of study and prayer, these ninety reflections on the Gospel of John provide a fresh understanding of Jesus' life and teaching.

Laurie weaves stories and images of Jesus with his signature humor and keen insight. The result is biblical depth presented in a clear, engaging style. In each reading you will discover who Jesus is and how to walk with him as the first disciples did.

BakerBooks
a division of Baker Publishing Group
Grand Rapids, Michigan